The Diary of a Poet

Chauntelle Madondo

BookLeaf
Publishing

Presentation by *BookLeaf Publishing*

Web: www.bookleafpub.com

E-mail: info@bookleafpub.com

ISBN: 9789357745598

First edition 2023

DEDICATION

I dedicate this book to my daughter Aiyana and my son Theo. My hope for you is that you will use your voice to speak your truth, express your feelings and stand up for what is right. Always remember how powerful your words are.

Proverbs 18:4 "<u>A person's words can be life-giving water</u>; words of true wisdom are as refreshing as a bubbling brook."

ACKNOWLEDGEMENT

I would like to give thanks to everyone who has supported my journey as a writer. You who come to support me at a live show. You who comment or send me a message about a video I post online. You who have spoken words of encouragement along the way. And to my family and friends who babysit my children, which enables me to chase after my dreams!

Most importantly, I would like to give thanks to God for blessing me with this gift of writing, understanding my feelings and being able to articulate them in poetic form. I also want to give thanks for the lessons learned and for His grace which kept me through it all.

Proverbs 12:18 "There is one who speaks rashly like the thrusts of a sword, but the tongue of the wise brings healing."

PREFACE

Growing up I was unsure of what and who I wanted to become. I was a shy child who found friendship in pens and paper, thus my purple *Groovy chick* diary became my confidant.

Zimbabwean born, moving to the UK aged nine, I was an outcast in my primary school and high school. Experiencing what I know now to be an identity crisis at such a young age, I began writing about my feelings. My introduction to Literature and poetry in high school was the catalyst of my poetic journey, which has since developed into Spoken word.

This collection of poems includes some personal pieces for people close to me, such as my dearest big sister Charlotte who sadly passed away on 24.07.2020 (I love you so much sis, I know you would be proud of me). Additionally, my friend Jabulani (Breeze) passed away a month before (16.06.2020), rest in eternal peace to you both.
I also explore love and healing and try to uplift with my work.

I hope you enjoy my first collection!
May God bless you and keep you well, thank you for reading.

Oh and one more thing…

Write your story! There is beauty in expression and sharing your vulnerable, true self.

January

Sometimes no one will come to save you
You have to be strong and save you
Sometimes survival is dependent on you
becoming your own savior
It may not always feel like we have choices but
we do
It's not only cars that have suicide doors life
does too
You decide whether you step through
It is a difficult decision as life can really shake
you and leave you shaken

Realities of life can cut like a sabre
Instead of giving up, speaking about your
feelings is safer
Speaking is releasing and healing - a safe haven
Life is precious. YOUR life is precious
Your life is sacred
So those suffering in silence I summon you to
speak
And those of you who are spoken to
I am begging you to listen

Therapy

When I meet someone who gives me a bit of
attention I attach
I begin to behave like Benjamin Button
reverting back to being a baby, and like a baby
to a breast I latch
Even if I know we are not compatible
I convince myself that our opposites attract
In fact we are a perfect match
That's when a plan predestined to fail begins to
hatch

I am with a man that God never intended me to
be with
Self inflicted pain, shame, heartbreak which all
could have been avoided if I wasn't so desperate
for love to begin with
It all begins with me
It all begins with my mind and self esteem
which has always been low

Maybe if my father hugged me more. Or at all.
Maybe if he told me he loved me, or I was
special
Maybe my search for love in man is intentional

To fill a void of emptiness that could only be
filled by a love that's parental
But I can't blame it all on daddy issues
So what else is the issue?
Silently soul searching for further issues

Therapy

Forgiveness

What does it mean to forgive?
To let go? To move on, to forget, to pray, to
hope, to love, to live?
Forgiving is dying to thy selfish needs of
righteousness
Putting someone else first
Because although forgiveness is healing, to
forgive can also hurt
Which is ironic as unforgiveness can be a curse
As much as it hurts to forgive, to not forgive can
feel worse

It is such a funny little thing
A healing little thing
It cleanses and frees and strengthens us within
It takes bravery and courage
Forgiveness is a seed planted which we must
water with grace and mercy for it to flourish

Forgiveness is similar to love
It is patient, it is kind. It does not envy, it does
not boast, it is not proud.
It is sometimes unjust, sometimes unfair
But remember..

When someone is crying to you desperate for
your forgiveness
One day.. You may be at the mercy of someone
else, begging for forgiveness
So forgive, forgive with joy
Free your heart, free your mind

Forgive

Baby Blue

All that time talking, teaching, tenaciously
tailoring, tongue-twisting, kissing, caressing,
caring, casually conversing, captivated closely
intertwined.
I fit so perfectly in your arms

The essence of your being made me calm
In the stillness, I searched the soul of this
scintillating man
Seeking sincerity. Seeking hope. Seeking to see
what was hidden beneath the surface
But you were ever so hard to read
Nevertheless, I solemnly swore that this feeling
was mutual. Swept off my feet I was so sure this
feeling was mutual.
But it was merely habitual

Where are you now?
I only see you when I look up and view the baby
blue sky

Why?

What is Love?

Love can take its time to grow
It can take a day to fall in love
Love will make you breathless
Love is limitless and endless

Love is unpredictable. Love is predictable.
Love is routine. Love is spontaneous
Love will make you love love
And love to be loved, we love to love those who
love us and it is so amazing
Love.. A warm blanket that covers you and
touches you and makes you feel.. wanted

Love will make you and break you at the same
time
It will give you a new sense of life, a reason to
live and within seconds rip you apart and make
you wish for death
Love is death
Love is life.. Love is affection, attention.. Love
is perfection, obsession. Love is contradiction,
Love is real. Love is fiction.
Love is patient, love is kind.
Love does not envy, love does not boast,

Love is not proud. Love does not dishonor
others, love is not self-seeking, it is selfish.
Love is not easily angered, it keeps no record of
wrongs.
Love keeps records and records of wrongs.
Love is a friend
Love is revenge. Love is vengeful.
Love does not delight in evil but rejoices with
the truth. always protects, always trusts, always
hopes, always perseveres. Love never fails.
Love fails.
We fail those we love
We love those who fail us
What an oxymoron
What a phenomenon

That thing we call

Love

Chemistry

We had chemistry.
Lesson four.
Out of all science, I found Chemistry the most
interesting.
I loved the concept of chemistry,
Two different chemicals coming together
An experiment. To see if a chemical reaction
will take place.
Some chemical reactions were positive.
This chemical reaction was negative
We had chemistry.
So I believed. I soon realised we did not
I must have got things mixed up!
Silly me.
Silly me for thinking we had chemistry in the
first place
Silly me for believing we had chemistry at all.

Maths

You + Me - the arguments = Success
Together we are 1, divide us by 2 making 2
halves = Equality
Multiply the cherished moments we share by 10
Measure the time spent in each other's presence
and increase it by 5%
You + I - the secrets = a closer bond
Find the mode of our lies and eliminate the
whole value
Find the missing angle of our friendship = less
mistakes made
You add I minus the Negativity = Longer lasting
relationship
Add more loyalty. More trust and increase the %
of smiles and compliments
You add I = happiness
You + I = greatness

Timeline

I see proposals, engagements and weddings on a
daily basis on my timeline
Life goals, Couple goals have me feeling like I
am running out of time
I am usually okay… most days…
I grasp the ability to be happy for "them"
Those who post about their belief in finding
love.
I am finding love -does not want to find me

I know I am not the only one who feels this way
I speak to so many broken hearts filled with
regret and torment over the pressures of social
media
Timelines of when and how to lose weight,
When to have a baby
When to buy a house, when you should have
your life figured out

We all have our own struggles to fit in
Big shoes we always try to fit in
Just be you.

And I know you're tired of hearing it but just do
you!
It's a short life and we only get one
Please do what makes you happy

Groundhog Day

Everyday feels the same
Different day, same pain
Using my last bit of strength to write this poem
for you
I wish I could say it to your face, but all I can do
is write this poem for you
My migraine has become a part of my being
So much so I hardly feel it

It's hard to hear my head pound when my heart
breaks so loud
I feel so empty and alone even in the midst of a
big crowd
I just want to hug, to hold you now

Come home, please come home right now
It's not fair what happened to you
I wish I could take your place in that grave, I
HATE what happened to you
Life has become a recurring nightmare I cannot
wake from

Why?
Everyday feels the same

Different day, same pain
Different day, the pain remains
They tell me time is a great healer and in time I
will forget
Their ignorance makes me so angry, how dare
they say I will forget!
You, I will never forget.
Each day is the same
Different day, still the pain

Grief

It takes 273 days, 9 months for new life to be
birthed into this world
Yet we expect its departure to be a quick process
Death and bereavement are the hardest things I
have ever to had to process
Stolen time.
We assume people move on and don't realise
reality is they've made little to no progress
Grief. It's a process
Apparently there are 5 stages
But I am not convinced because in 5 months I
have mentally fought through more than 5
phases
Glued to my bed in the discomfort of my own
home
My mind has traveled to far more than 5 places
Nothing makes sense like sentences with just
words and no spaces
How on earth do I face this??
Drowned in deep waters of regret which
regularly remind me of the debt that I can never
repay

There is no method or one specific way to grieve
All you can do is try
You may find yourself suddenly getting angry or
tearful for no reason
Feeling stone cold in the midst of a storm even
in the summer season
Self-sabotaging anything good because how dare
I enjoy life and have good times when a loved
one is in a grave?
How dare I run from opportunities when they
were so brave?
Life steals life with no remorse and sometimes
with no warning
Life steals mornings and leaves us in mourning

So what do you do?
Just wake up, have a shower or a bath
Get dressed
That's all you have to do, the rest of it will
follow
Grieving is a process that can last for years so
get through today, don't worry about tomorrow.
Just know that they are proud of you!
And want you to do well
The body to hold and hug is gone
But forever and ever their spirit lives on
Hold on to the goodness of their existence,
remember them in all you do

Never forget how much they love you.
And remember

There is no method or one specific way to grieve
So just grieve, the pain may never go away, but
somehow, in time,
The burden will miraculously ease

Charlotte

Though no longer here in the flesh, your spirit
lives
That's the only thing that's giving me some sense
of peace
You are always with us in our hearts
Although you feel far, we are never apart
You are free of this world's pain and sorrow
But you were taken far too soon, I wish we still
had another tomorrow

There are many things Charlotte was..
There are many things Charlotte is.
There are many things I will never understand
But what I do know is this..

Charlotte was and is loved and cherished
Your absence has left a hole and a permanent
scar. That is indisputable
Charlotte was and is.. In ALL of its meaning
Simply and truly
Beautiful.

Breeze

I am not the best swimmer
But I would desperately and diligently swim
down the deepest sea just to see your face again
I would hold my breath until I turned blue just to
be with you and dwell in your presence

I am not the best athlete
But I would run, run and keep on running,
rapidly rushing to wherever you are just to tell
you I love you.
I wish you knew how much I love you.
I don't think you did.
But I do, always will.

Thank you for calling me friend
There is only one thing that puts me at ease
And that's knowing that you are now resting in
peace
Every time the wind blows and I feel a breeze
That cool, calm, sweet soothing breeze, I'll know
it's you.
And I will stop for a moment and smile..
Remembering you

Mother

Mother. You brought me into this world
Introduced me to land
Born in the motherland
I am blessed you are my mother and
Blessed to be a part of you
Blessed that I resemble you

Warrior strength, you overcome
Battles fought that you have won
Still you rise and fight for your children
Working hard since I was an infant
In fact, I only saw your strength when I got
older, wiser
A teacher, nurse, caregiver, provider

Unique, My Queen, you reign supreme
Divine, sublime, one of a kind.
I am blessed, I am honored that you are mine
I am overjoyed that you are my
Mother.

Aiyana

When a seed is planted, it first grows roots
And so it is you were rooted in me
My beautiful flower I watched grow from 2
stripes on a stick to a body with limbs
From hearing your heartbeat within
To hearing your first cry out loud
I am proud.

 Every time I look into your eyes
I am bound by your beauty. Completely
captivated, continuously connected, my blood
runs through your veins, my cheerful chosen
child
The joy you bring.

Just 6 years in, feels only like a moment has
passed
Such a phenomenon how babies grow so fast
From Crawling to talking to walking
From smiling to winning to sulking
Your terrible twos were terrific
It's incredible, you're so terrific
Perfect.. To be specific

I thank God for the blessing you are.
Not just to me, but to others you are..
So fascinating, fabulous, fearless, friendly,
funny, how fortunate we are!
Receiving the most precious flower that never
dies.
Aiyana: a beautiful flower that eternally
blossoms
May you continue to blossom and shine

Theo

Your morning began with mourning
With cry of life leaving your body and filling the
room
So small but you filled out the room
Not sure how you fit in my womb
A miracle!
The beginning of life is incredible!
Unfathomable.
Like a sunrise
Or looking directly into the sun's eyes
I look into my son's eyes..
And see glory.
Beauty in the sound of my son's cries

Black boy
You are blessed beyond belief you will see
As you get older and wiser
You are destiny's child which means you're a
survivor
You are not those things the media portrays you
to be
You are perfect black boy
Be anything you want to be!
Son, shine. The sky is no limit for you

Affirmation

Repeat this
Believe this

My life is important and very precious I am
grateful for what I have and not jealous
I am brave and confident
I will overcome obstacles
My personality is wonderful
I am ME and oh so beautiful!
I can do anything! I am powerful
I am worthy, I am valuable
I am determined and successful
I am loved

I am me which is my power
I am courageous and fearless
I am.
I am perfectly me.

A poem for Black Women

Beautiful beginnings
You were beautiful from the beginning
You are faithful and loyal.
You are royal! You don't need to walk around
with an actual crown for it to show
It's just obvious from the way the sun makes
your melanin skin glow
It's like gold and it's beyond me!
The way you are so dark and lovely
Like diamond refined, Perfectly designed
Perfect in every way you could never be ugly!

Black don't crack - it's a fact- we shine!
Maybe because we use vaseline in the Winter
time
Maybe because our skin pops in the
Summertime
And when we walk we have a Spring in our step.
It's so awesome, we are just like Autumn the
way leaves fall from trees but regrow the next
season.
We fall, but our downfall is only for a season for
we regrow and blossom brightly shining in
everything we do

I love being a black girl, black girl, do you??
I am my biggest fan
I love me as I am.
Black girls grow up using blue magic
Not knowing they have that black girl magic
Be proud
Be confident
You are not aggressive and loud
You are passionate
Not angry
You are compassionate
Not masculine and manly

You are not angry and aggressive like the media
portrays u to be
No you are calm and serene
Like the master's peace
You, beautifully and wonderfully made like a
masterpiece.
You do not need to wear a mask to please

"You are enough"

A poem for Single moms

Single moms
Those working the morning shift, day shift into
night shift with low pay
Lack of sleep and backache is the only wage
Delicately decorated in the decadence of vomit
stains
Heavy heartedly hustling hard to secure a good
future for your children
It's work and no play
Can't keep up with dates everyday seems the
same

Can't relax because nappies need to be changed
Beds need to be made
Carpet cleaning
Cobwebbed ceiling
Bins need to be taken out in the evening
Dishes need to be done
A job for two is being done by one
It's hard being a single mum!

And when the curtains go up and you're stood
center stage
They will shout insults at you and make you feel
ashamed
Make YOU feel ashamed
Because the father of your child walked away?
There is a stigma attached and it's so strange
When it comes to men, the reaction is not the
same
Single fathers are highly praised.
And no, It is not a competition
Because both parents should be there for their
children
If you're a single parent be proud
You are strong.
You mask your dependence
You have mastered independence
The next time you look down on a single mom,
Don't.

Speak your Truth

Some call me a poet, some call me an artist
All I know is I put my heart on the page and
hope that someone who sees this or reads this
can relate

There is great power in words
Words change lives
So it may be uncomfortable to share but words
bring light

You and I may never verbally converse
But still spiritually connect through a piece or
verse
With the words
I speak
I see.. You and I are not that different
Only difference is I speak

Your truth
Beauty lies in the vulnerable you
Be vulnerable too
Share your story and speak your truth

Love leaves

Love leaves hearts vacant
Empty rooms of what used to be
That familiar scent that lingers and visits from
time to time when love is gone
To remind us of what once was

Yes... It is true

Love leaves hearts vacant
Which means there is room
For new beginnings, for new Love
Though change is hard
And letting go is painful
Life continues to bring forth new hopes
New opportunities, new possibilities
Through new Love

Open the door of your heart
When love knocks
For you never know the journey ahead
The lessons to be learnt
Always make room

For love

Black Lives Matter

Earth quake! I can feel the Earth is shaken

Because another innocent life of a black man has
been taken
And now another family of a black man has a
permanent empty space in their hearts that will
forever remain vacant
And now another black man's future is forsaken
And now another trip to the shop to buy flowers
to lay down on the pavement
And now another murderer wearing the SAME
clothes with the SAME badge is being excused
when their guilt is SO blatant
And now another Black King killed
And now another Black King stolen by the
Justice System which acts as a double agent
Acting as gods abusing their power like Satan
Evil.

There are far too many evil beings
For far too long it's been the blind leading the
blind but it's time, way over time the blind start
seeing

Hardened hearts need to be softened it's time
they start feeling
So if we must protest.. And show them the vivid
images and bombard them with videos that they
deem grotesque
So be it. This time they WILL see it.
This time.. Enough is enough.

Enough police brutality beating black bodies
leaving them bleeding
Enough white privilege ignoring racism like its
non-existent
It hurts in my heart so bad I can feel it
I am hurt. I am tired. I am broken to pieces
Because another black man is in a grave
When he should still be breathing.